Trying to Knit

by Natalie Lambert
illustrated by Carol Heyer

Practice Decodable 68

I0805983

McGraw Hill Education

Bothell, WA • Chicago, IL • Columbus, OH • New York, NY

MHEonline.com

Send all inquiries to:
McGraw-Hill Education
8787 Orion Place
Columbus, OH 43240

ISBN: 978-0-02-144964-4
MHID: 0-02-144964-3

Printed in China.

8 9 10 11 12 DSS 27 26 25 24 23

A lot of kids want to knit, but they don't know how. Knitting is hard!

In the beginning, I could not knit at all. My knitting looked like knots.

At first, I designed mittens to knit. I did not knit them well. My knuckles did not fit!

I knitted heavy socks. They reached my knees!

I knitted a sweater. It looked neat. And then I had a knack for knitting.

I am in a knitting club. Knock! Knock! I must go. The knitting club needs my knitting know-how!